Dancing Soul

Dancing Soul: The Voice of Spirit Evolving
Copyright 1995 © By Gwen Randall-Young

All rights reserved. Printed in Canada. No part of this book may be used or reproduced in any manner whatsoever without written permission from the Publisher. For information address:
DANCING SOUL PRODUCTIONS
P.O. Box 80057
Broadmoor P.O.
82 Athabascan Avenue
Sherwood Park, Alberta
Canada T8A 5T1
Telephone: (403) 464-8533 Fax: (403) 464-5503

FIRST EDITION

Published by:

DANCING SOUL PRODUCTIONS
A Division of Gwen Randall - Young
Psychological Services Ltd.
P.O. Box 80057
Broadmoor P.O.
82 Athabascan Avenue
Sherwood Park, Alberta
Canada T8A 5T1

Cover Art By Matthew Brett
Graphic Design & Layout By Dawn Makarowski

Canadian Cataloguing in Publication Data

Randall - Young, Gwen, (date)
  Dancing Soul

  ISBN 1-896578-00-4

  I. Title.
  PS8585.A34D36 1995   C818'.54   C95-910656-1
  PR9199.3.R36D36 1995

Dancing Soul

The Voice of Spirit Evolving

Gwen Randall-Young

*This book is dedicated to
Jordy, Jessalyn and Tasha,
the beautiful souls
who chose me to be their mother.*

Acknowledgements

To acknowledge those who have supported the creation of this book is to thank those who have contributed to the evolution of my soul. That would include everyone who has touched my life. As for the latest stage, out of which these writings have emerged, there are some who deserve special mention. Since it all began in Maui, Hawaii, I must thank:
Romy, who has taught me so much about miracles;
Prageet, who opened the doors;
Sian, who always believes that anything is possible;
Alan, who will always be special to me because he is
   such a clear and loving reflection; and,
Andrea, special friend and beautiful soul.

It was *Gary* who was most instrumental in encouraging me to listen to my higher self, and to give voice to Solara III. She emerged clearly as we sat high atop Halcakala Crater. Haleakala means "House of the Sun" and only later did I realize the profound significance of what had transpired, and the appropriateness of Solara speaking there. Through Gary, I learned reverence for the mysteries of non-physical reality. Thank you Gary, for easing my transition and for urging me to write.

Acknowledgement and thanks also to:
Cheryl Lee, for her unfailing love and support;
Rose Chambers, a dear angel who shines brightly;
Marv and Nan, for bringing me into the world;
Barbara, for enthusiastically supporting me in all
   that I do;

David, for always knowing who I really was;
Nadine, who left this Earth long ago, but never left me;
Aunty Mae, for her unconditional, joyful loving;
Merv and Joy, who are always there for me;
Ashley, for being such a big help and a lovely spirit;
Dawn, for all her hard work and dedication to this book;
Maureen and Fred, who helped me tremendously to get here;
Jan, a most special soul whose love and support I cherish;
Douglas Yakimetz, for never giving up;
All of my *clients*, who trust me with their hearts and souls.
    You are so beautiful and your trust is a gift. I
    love every one of you.
Winston, who challenged me to live my truth;
Terry, for being a very special father;
Jordy, for being such a special son, for seeing my soul
    and for helping to create miracles;
Jessy, for being the beautiful, independent spirit that you
    truly are and for all you teach me;
Tasha, for the delightful, loving energy that radiates freely
    from your soul - you are an angel;
Melonie, a most gentle, warm and loving spirit whose
    encouragement, competence and hard work turned
    these writings into a book. It wouldn't have happened
    without you, Mel.
John, a very rare and precious being who knew I was out
    there and trusted the Universe to help him find me.
    You truly are the wind beneath my wings.
And finally, to *you*, the reader, and the wonderful energy
    that has now brought us together. I honor the light within
    you. May it always shine brightly.

Dancing Soul

*Time seems to weave
the tapestry of our lives,
and yet we know
that time
is an illusion.*

*It is the inner core of our being
that is moving,
gently,
slowly
through its own
unique
dance.*

How are we to grasp the meaning, the essence of the timeless flow through eternity? In the cosmic realm, such a question would not make any sense at all. It would be like asking what is the meaning of a river, or a rock. It is a limited consciousness that tries to picture the Great Wall of China by examining a specimen of rock from that wall, while sitting somewhere thousands of miles away. It cannot be done. One must see a picture of the whole, or travel to China.

*To really understand,
we must relinquish our limited perspective,
and accept that true understanding
requires a totally different experience.*

*We must shift
to a higher octave
of experiencing.*

Only the wise ones remember the way back to the One. They have prepared themselves for this time when they must assist others into new awareness, into light. They require certain experiences themselves, to boost them into the higher octaves.

*Being open to receive
　　　is the highest priority
　　　　　for growth and learning.*

Holding on to current perceptions of how things are, is akin to insisting on using a horse and cart when air travel is possible. We must release the old ways of seeing the world.

*It is not the world that is changing,
it is our consciousness
that is expanding.*

It is possible to move in and out of different levels of consciousness as easily as one changes clothing. Inner essence is constant regardless of the level of consciousness that is chosen. Most people wear clothing that reflects how they see themselves, and similarly adopt a level of consciousness that reflects their understanding of being.

*Those who experience expanded awareness
can beckon others forward,
however only those who have created
enough inner awareness
and stillness
to hear the call
will move forward.*

The call is like a magnet; a steady persistent pull in the direction of growth and awareness. There is a signal for each of us, and some of us wake up to it, while others may go an entire lifetime oblivious, the way one sleeps through a ringing alarm clock. Many resist waking up, because it feels so much easier to remain asleep. However, waking up is a process that brings energy and excitement to our journey, so that we become more fully alive. It is a rebirth of consciousness so that we begin to see the world and life experience in an entirely new way.

Deep in the recesses of our soul is the memory that rekindles our desire to proceed along the path of our soul's journey.

It is easy, on this planet, to become sidetracked, because the energy here is so dense. It is a little like a cosmic quicksand, or a drug that slows us down. But waves of energy have been, and continue to stimulate a process of awakening in many.

These waves are the signals that are being directed towards us from the non-space, non-time dimensions.

It is possible to be aware of coexistence in these other dimensions while present in the Earth plane, and many on the planet are now doing this.

They serve as the interpreters, or translators of the next stage in our evolution. They have been writing, speaking, or expressing themselves through art and music, to slowly bring new energies into our awareness. This is a preparation or conditioning for the shifts that are to come. Many see the shifts as being marked by chaos and confusion, but it is very possible to manifest a smooth transition, like an airplane that lands so softly that you're surprised to find yourself on the ground. There is no great effort required to make the transition. We need only become like the plant that turns towards the sun.

We turn our consciousness towards truth and compassion, and the process naturally unfolds.

If we stubbornly resist, then we choose a life of struggle, pain and darkness. Gradually, like the plant, we wither away, and others can virtually see the life draining out of us, regardless of our age. If, on the other hand, we choose the light, we remain radiant and alive at every stage of life. We all know people who are choosing darkness, and people who are choosing light.

The "light beings" seem to thrive, no matter what tragedies may befall them, and those in the dark seem unable to find joy, no matter how much they seem to have going for them.

As you are reading this, there is an opportunity for you to expand your awareness regardless of how evolved or unevolved you perceive yourself to be. Even the most evolved among us have a long way to go. No doubt the owners of the first automobiles thought that they had reached the apex of transportation.

*But within
us
lie the very seeds
of our own awakening
and transformation.*

Within each of us lies an infinite untapped potential,
a cosmic time release capsule.

As inhabitants of the Earth, we are in the process of a "coming of age". Like the adolescent experiencing the surge of unfamiliar hormones, at times we may seem confused and disoriented, as we try to determine what is truly "real".

Learning at every stage of life is a function of experience, and the more we experience, the broader is our understanding.

We may never have total understanding, but like the Universe, our collective consciousness is forever expanding.

The Message

A message began coming to me in Maui, Hawaii, in 1990. It was as though someone was speaking to me, but there was no sound. Words came into my consciousness, carried by an energy that I could not ignore. The words, "I am Solara III", initially prefaced the messages. I wondered if this was a dream, or perhaps something pathological, and yet from the outset I sensed that there was deep wisdom and goodness in this energy. Everything in my mind rejected the possibility that this could be happening, and at first I tried to ignore it, hoping it would go away. I kept it pretty much to myself, sharing it only with a couple of evolved souls who assured me that this was a valid experience, and I developed a reverence for the process. I decided to record some of what I was receiving, much out of curiosity. I tucked it away and almost forgot about it, until one day recently when I was telling a friend about this experience. She was interested in seeing the writing. Looking at it, it became clear that it comprised an important message, complete within itself. Interspersed within the text, like a musical interlude, is the beautiful energy of "Dancing Soul".

Dancing Soul puts the words of the message to music: her words invite an integration or alignment of intellect and emotion with the knowing of soul.

The writing is a guide to linking the energies of the physical with the non-physical realms. We have the ability to access energy or information from the higher realms, but we have to step outside of ego or mind in order to express this energy. The potential for harnessing electrical, nuclear or solar energy was always there. All that was needed was to develop a means to access that energy. So it is with the energy of cosmic unconsciousness. Solara III and Dancing Soul are expressions of my higher self as it tunes into that higher consciousness. Expressed as personified energies, they serve as a link connecting human consciousness, and cosmic consciousness. This process is a manifestation of an evolutionary shift. As humans we have seen the shift from tribal village to global village. There is a similar shift evolving within consciousness, as we grow from members of the Planetary tribe to members of the Universal tribe. Solara III and Dancing Soul resonate from that place that comprises the higher selves of all of us, that place where we are all one. It is with love that I share this special part of me, so that it may serve as a mirror reflecting that part of you also.

May we all be Dancing Souls,
celebrating this Dance of Life.

The Awakening

As I began to become comfortable tuning in to higher consciousness, it felt almost as though I was climbing a mountain. As I moved upwards, not only did I see all that was below with greater clarity, but I now had a vantage point from which it seemed I could see forever. It was not so much a "seeing", as it was a knowing, and this knowing came into my consciousness as words, which flowed effortlessly. On one occasion, when I was "being" in that energy of Solara III, I felt a much stronger, more powerful energy moving through my consciousness. It interrupted the flow that I was in, as though to bring an important message. It said:

> *"We speak to you from Beyond the Beyond. We have waited for the opening in the energy field that is the higher self. We now wish to communicate from beyond the 11th dimension. There are many who may serve as transmitters from the closer dimensions, however very few are connected to the Beyond. We are the Eyes of*

the Aeons, and we have been watching. We see that it is time to increase the vibrational level on your planet, and we see that this is not occurring at the present level of human consciousness. We have chosen to provide assistance rather than to allow nature to take its course, for the survival of your planet and the evolution of its people serves a higher purpose in the Eternal realms.

We are directing energy from the Beyond towards some of the souls in your dimension. These souls are beings who recognize their purpose and have agreed to serve this higher purpose. They are assisting in reconnecting souls to the One. As you begin to recognize the Universal energy within, and to blend that energy with the souls of others, you shall begin your journey homeward. When energies are blended in this way, there is a power which is far beyond what the souls themselves have brought to the union. It is this power which opens the way to the Eternal realms. Few however, are yet brave enough to stay with this vision, and instead retreat from this energy. They may think that they have had a peak experience, or a feeling of heart opening, but they do not yet realize that this is their essence they are experiencing. You are love."

I was both moved and mystified by this energy that felt more profound than anything I have experienced. Although it defied explanation, it was nonetheless clear that these words established a context for all that was to come. My understanding was that I could receive this energy at the level of higher self, and it would be translated into a form that could be communicated to others. The sharing of this energy would assist in expanding the collective consciousness. And so it is that I allow the words of Solara III and Dancing Soul to grace the pages of this book.

Awareness: Beyond the Beyond

Within every soul is knowledge of the whole. Surprisingly, much energy is required to keep this knowingness *out* of awareness. Many of your activities including schooling, audio and video entertainment, and even some religious training, serve to keep you from knowing who you really are. You are trained to believe that your mind is like a vessel which must be filled up in order to function or to know. In fact, your mind is like a two way transmitter/receiver. Knowingness does not reside within the mind, but rather flows through it. It is the knowingness which is the essence. It is as though the mind functions as a radio: disconnected from source, the radio is nothing but plastic and some wires. If a radio ceases to function, the source is not affected. It simply continues to pass through other functioning channels.

To continue with the analogy, many on Earth keep the volume on their transmitter so low that they cannot hear anything. Others keep so much "noise" in their lives that they cannot hear. Some have begun to tune in a little here and there, and of course others have discovered their infinite capacity to receive. These are your channels, who willingly share what they are hearing. Some channel music, or art, and this is because words do not exist in other dimensions, and so these people channel what they experience. Color and sound are a more appropriate language for the soul. In fact, your language severely limits your ability to receive unless you are prepared to allow yourself to totally receive the energies that are there, and then to translate in a way that expands your current concepts of reality.

Many of you are beginning to have the experience of receiving energies in this way. It is as though entities such as Solara III are delighting in projecting energy towards your soul. What this is in fact is her soul, or Universal Oneness, moving out to surround you with loving essence, which allows your soul to experience itself somewhat apart from you. It is like the mother bird's loving push of the young out of the nest. You enjoy the sensation of being weightless, without the weight of the world, but do not yet believe that you could stay out there for long without falling. This is the beginning of awakening. You cannot fall.

Beyond the Beyond is the realm of total silence and perfect stillness. There is no moving to or passing through.

There is a perfect balance of the energies, as when two powerful magnets are drawn together. There is of course incredible power within this balance, and this is the energy which supports all that is. From the 11th dimension we can see infinitely in all directions. It is from this point that we draw the energies back to the Source. Infinity exists in all directions, and there is a continual flow of energy outward from Source, and then back again. Balance is constantly maintained. Your Universe and all that you know have been, until now, in a position of receiving energy, and in fact are manifestations of this outflow of energy. At the peak of the outflow the manifestations look as though they are separate entities, be they people or planets. Now, however, the energy is shifting, and it is the beginning of the return flow. Now the manifestations will begin to merge back into the One. The energy that is you will thus merge into the whole, and will then become part of the outflow in another direction, which will in turn manifest in other forms, depending on the configuration of the energy patterns.

Change

Pain does not exist in the higher dimensions. Pain is often the form we choose to give to change. For change to occur, a shift of some kind is necessary. It may be a physical change, a shift in energy, or a change in perception. Pain comes when we resist change: when we attempt to prevent a necessary shift. Pain serves to prevent one from continuing in a state of denial.

However, denial is often intensified, and so the pain must increase in frequency or intensity until the being has responded to its message. Pain is not something to be consciously avoided, for that would be to block awareness. However, it is possible to reduce pain by simply allowing change, and to recognize when change is necessary. Part of your evolutionary shift will see beings creating change in their lives before it appears necessary, rather than drifting into it and responding after the fact.

Enlightenment

Beyond thought is before thought. Thought is the last step in the transmission of energies through the dimensions. On your plane, it is generally believed that all thought is created within the mind. However, this would be like thinking that all the music that there is, is what one hears on the radio.

Music comes from many different sources. Listening to the radio is being more removed from the source, while listening to a live orchestral performance is being much closer to the source. What the composer hears in his or her mind *before the music is even written,* brings us still closer to source, but notice now there is a qualitative difference in the meaning of the word "source".

Much of what we hear in our minds is what might be called functional thought - ideas formulated within consciousness to allow us to maintain daily living. There is another form of thought which consists of creating the expression, via language, to convey or interpret a non-physical energy. This energy is a knowingness or awareness that is just there, and that we can intuit, whether or not we can put it into words. This is a cosmic consciousness that simply exists, and does not originate within our minds. It is an energy that comes from Source, in the most profound sense. What begins as a pulse of energy travels through the different dimensions, absorbing aspects of the various energies and releasing others. The energy becomes increasingly dispersed as it moves farther from Source, and thought is the manifestation of this energy at its outermost point. This energy interacts with human consciousness in its awakened form, thus producing a cosmic synergy which is the energy of creation. This energy may then be turned back towards Source, reconnecting with other energies on the homeward path, thus gaining strength and momentum.

Many of these energies are beginning to spontaneously vibrate in harmony, and this is what is being experienced as an increase in the vibrational frequency on your planet. It is an interactive Universe, a dance between individual and cosmic consciousness, which leaves neither the same as before.

We are evolving and creating at the same time: simultaneously the created and the creator. Grasping an understanding of, and learning to work with this process is one form of enlightenment. As we have said, this process leaves neither side unchanged. When you move into this dance, and feel a sense of lightness in your being, this is because at a cellular level, shifts from form (density) into energy are occurring. You are evolving into a light being.

Energy

All communication is energy transmission, reception, resistance or blockage. Beings may experience a harmonious exchange of loving energy, and when this occurs there is then more than the sum of individual energies. This is how beings grow and evolve, for all growth requires energy beyond that needed for maintenance. When loving energy is not transmitted to a being, or the being is unreceptive or resistive, growth is blocked. If the energy is not transmitted in a form that the being can utilize or decode as loving energy, optimal growth does not occur. Spiritual nutrients exist in abundance on your planet. Beings who evolve most quickly are those who are open and receptive, and can therefore absorb these nutrients. The learning, for this time, is to perceive the loving abundance in the Universe and to invite it into one's life, and to recognize that each individual is not only a receiver but also a transmitter. As energies are absorbed, beings can also allow the loving energy to flow outward to others, and thus enhance the evolution of the species.

Recognize the most potent energizers of your spirit within your life, and honor them. Give yourself the gift of connection to these essences, for it is through them that you connect with the higher energies of the other dimensions.

Experiencing Soul Essence

Such excitement is building as souls begin their homeward journey. Many of you are experiencing dramatic changes in how you see your life and purpose on this planet. As you surrender to the inner knowing, much energy is set free and thus raises the vibration of the energy around your planet. We have begun to show you the way of Beyond the Beyond. It is possible for you to experience that space and we shall try to describe how this is so. You must surrender your beliefs about finite space and time, and know that as you can dream or imagine about some future event, so you can project your awareness into that part of your soul that experiences Beyond the Beyond. Many of you, when trying first to meditate, could maintain empty mind for only brief periods, before being aware that thoughts had entered consciousness again. It is the same with projecting your awareness more fully into soul, but perhaps even more difficult to sustain the experience, for it requires movement completely out of the density of consciousness as you know it. When you are able to experience soul completely as essence, you have entered the zone of the Beyond. For many souls this does not occur until physical death has freed the soul from the confines of the body and third dimensional consciousness. It is a little like soul travel, but only a little, for in soul travel there is still the experience of time and space. We are given the ability to transcend these, but this ability is much like the untapped potential of the brain. Only a very minute portion of awareness is generally utilized on the Earth plane. Thus, when deeper awareness produces expanded perception, it is referred to as "Supernatural" or "Paranormal". What has been called natural or normal is simply the lowest common denominator of shared perception on your planet.

I am Dancing Soul
I have danced through time
And space
And around the edges
Of souls who could not
Would not
Let me in
And I have also danced
To the music of the Universe
And with souls who knew
My dance
Because
The ecstasy
And lightness
Of the dance
Reminded them
Of home
And sometimes even
Awakened
A sleeping heart.

Love

What is love? Love has been romanticized, and is often thought of as being the result of intention, but this is as absurd as suggesting that the sun *intends* to cast light on your planet. Light is simply there, and is vital to physical life. Love is the spiritual counterpart of light. It is simply there, and is vital for the existence and growth of the spirit. It is for us to allow it to flow, and to receive it. All illness and dysfunction are a result of blockage either in expressing or receiving love. Love of course flows from Source, and returns to Source. Source may be known as "The One", "Universal Flow", "God" or any other such term. The terminology is not important, as words are only required when Souls are not vibrating with Source, and communication must be assisted. When this occurs, it is as though the experience is removed from the soul, and reconstructed on a different plane where it is only a very crude and limited representation. This is why beings often experience communication difficulties, and also why there is such a strong connection with souls of similar vibration. The more similar the vibration, the more direct and non-verbal is communication. In fact, more of the communication becomes a type of energy exchange, and there is less reliance on words to share experience.

I am Dancing Soul
And I can take you
To a place where
Souls can merge
And fully experience
The essence of another
Like inhaling
The fragrance of a flower
Or allowing music
To flow around and
Through you
Almost like
You have been the flower
Or the melody
Except that you can
Return to your essence
And hold those other
Essences
Within your soul
And you have
Expanded in knowing
And loving them.

Life Force

There is also another kind of love, and that is the passionate form of energy that can be called "life force". This is a much more focused and intense form of loving energy, much as there is always moving air on the Earth, but sometimes it takes the form of strong winds, even hurricanes or tornadoes. Strong passion can be similarly destructive when one becomes blinded by the passion, or if the energy is misdirected. However, it is an incredibly positive force that is the power of creation. It is like the booster rocket that can lift one out of the gravity of Earth consciousness. Many are afraid of their passion, and seek always to control it. This may cause illness, depression, and lack of energy. Others do not realize that this incredible power is there for the purpose of creating, expanding and evolving the expression of who we are. They may direct the energy in obsessive ways, acting out with drugs, alcohol, sex, or overworking, thinking that this will somehow relieve the pressure of this energy. The Universe is trying to push humans to give birth to the full expression of their essence. Not understanding what is required, individuals seek various distractions, which ultimately are never satisfying. The passionate energy that is life force is the energy of growth, the manifestation of the soul's desire for expansion. It is important to recognize this energy for what it is: to learn to work, play or dance with it, allowing spirit to move naturally, the way the body might spontaneously move to music. Life force may seek expression through creative activities, including art, music, dance or writing. It might be expressed through gardening, parenting, playing with the dog or doing scientific research. Aligning with the energy of life force means finding out what you love, what brings you joy, and doing it. This is the way to incorporate cosmic energy into the process of co-creating our being. There is much of this intense, loving energy in the other dimensions, the difference being that it is not an unusual phenomenon, but rather is the norm. It is because of repression and holding back that those occasions when one feels totally aligned with life force are called "peak experiences" on your planet.

I dwell in Dancing Soul
I am the fire of the Sun
And I come to awaken you
To the passion that lies
Deep within your being
I will ignite it
So that you can feel
Waves
Radiating out
To the very edges of
Your soul
And back to
Your center
So that every
Stream
Of your consciousness
Reflects
The glowing embers
Of passion experienced
And remembered.

Healing

One of the purposes of the journey through life is healing. Many spend years, or an entire lifetime, unaware that there is any more to them than the mind and body. The soul is neglected; separated from conscious awareness. This means that the self does not have access to the nurturing qualities of soul. It is a little like a child feeling lost in the woods because he cannot see his mother right there behind a nearby tree. Access to soul is always readily available, but if one is unaware of this, there is an experience of loneliness and alienation. The individual may conclude from these feelings that he or she is unworthy and thus reject self. This creates deep pain, which can also manifest as physical illness. It is an imbalance that ultimately can only be resolved by healing the relationship between body, mind and soul. Turmoil in life may be a reflection of the struggle between these different aspects as they move towards integration.

I am Dancing Soul
And I can heal the wounds
Of separation
I can gather up
The scattered parts
Of shattered wholeness
There
Like the petals of
A delicate rose
Carelessly tossed
By the winds
Of some other
Storm
I can re-create
And rearrange
All parts of being
To create a new
Expression
Of the essence
That was always there.

*And like a subtle
Fragrance
That lingers on
The essence
Is never lost
Only transformed
And held
In whatever form
Is chosen
To best reflect
Those aspects
Which are
Eternal.*

So dance with me
And feel the healing
At every level
Of your being
Let the balm
Of my love
Soothe you
Surround you
As you become
New
Once again.

Relationship

When two people are drawn into relationship there is a focused concentration of energy. The purpose of all relationship is learning, so there is an energy flow between those who have something to learn from, or with, each other. Sometimes the learning is joyful, other times painful, but always there is learning. Other people are reflections of aspects of self. At the level of soul there is perfect understanding; it is on the level of self that struggle and difficulty arise. The direction of the evolutionary path is towards being in loving relationship with all other beings, meaning viewing and relating with others from the stance of acceptance and compassion. The farther one is from this stance, the greater the level of difficulty in the relationship. The self may instinctively produce behaviors that will push away those who will not honor its soul. This is often the reason that children distance from parents. If parents want their children to be replicas of themselves, it is because they do not realize that each child is a soul on his or her own journey. To preserve the integrity of the soul's path, separation occurs between parent and child. Such separation is avoided when the soul is honored. It is only the physical and intellectual being that is childlike at a young age, not the soul. A child's soul may be older, more evolved than that of its parents.

Similarly, such separation may occur within couples, so that the apparent conflicts over finances, communication or children, for example, is really a reflection of the deeper struggle to connect at the level of soul. The soul knows its path, but until there is an integration between soul and self, there may be a pulling in opposite directions which manifests, in life, as struggle.

The purpose of soul level communication in relationship is not to control or change the thoughts and feelings of the other, but instead to understand, to try to know what it feels like, to be that other person. It is to share perceptions, as you might do with someone from another culture, with interest and openness, but without judgment. This widening of the circle of acceptance expands the awareness of each soul, and raises the vibrational level of the relationship.

A relationship that recognizes soul is a powerful opportunity for learning. Think of a seed, in which resides the complete potential for ultimate growth and development. Given a nurturing environment, its essence naturally unfolds. So it is in relationships between loving souls. The concentrated combination of energies that is created upon coming together is the nucleus from which all that can be will evolve.

It is for each being simply to be open and aware of what is flowing through essence, and to lovingly accept whatever comes into awareness, without trying to change it, or to resist its flow. To try to resist or control what comes is to stunt and distort the growth of all that can be. The energy then becomes blocked, and erupts sporadically in dysfunctional ways, causing emotional or physical distress.

Awakening within humans now is the urge for expansion, which is a part of the natural unfolding and joining of loving essence for the homeward journey. This creates a craving for the intense and unconditional loving which the unconscious is beginning to remember. Without the realization that this love *is* essence, full and complete within each being, there often follows one or a series of frustrating attempts to fulfill this craving in relationship with another. It is not for a couple to "create" this wonderful state of harmonious loving between them, but rather to allow their own loving essences to flow towards the other. In combining the loving essences, the vibration created permits a joining with the Universal loving essence.

Spontaneous joy and recognition is sometimes felt between two souls regardless of the nature of the Earth relationship. This is a natural flow of loving energy, not to be confused with sexual energy, and it is possible to feel it with all other beings, for we are of one essence. Illusions of separateness often prevent this kind of loving soul connection. When it is felt, it is because the individuals have allowed themselves to flow into that particular moment and surrender to what is. It is in the surrendering that the openness to receive is created.

I am Dancing Soul
And I have come
To awaken
Sleeping hearts.
I will wrap
My loving essence
Around your soul
And whisper
A melody
That only your heart
Can hear
And at first
The melody will seem
Only vaguely
Familiar
But in time
It will become
A part of the melody
Of your own heart
Indistinguishable
From Source
And an infinite
Link
To all that is.

Letting Go

One of the strongest reflex actions of the newborn human is to close its fists very tightly. This is done in an attempt to hold firmly to itself and to become less vulnerable. This response is carried into adult life, although not always on a physical level. It is more of an emotional or psychological contraction in response to perceived threat to the equilibrium of the organism. This is a response that serves survival and maintenance of the individual, but in maintaining the equilibrium, it often blocks growth. For whenever change occurs, there is by definition a shift in the equilibrium of the system. Humans often hold on very tightly to situations or beliefs long past the point when they have ceased to be served by them. Holding on keeps one bound to one spot.

On the other hand, each "letting go" moves one into another level of ever expanding circles of awareness. Because "letting go" can be so difficult and often painful, many do it once in a lifetime, and feel that in so doing they have achieved enlightenment. True growth and evolution come with the recognition that it is not for us to hold on to anything, but rather to let the energies of life experiences simply flow through us. This flow cleanses and purifies the soul, which is what is meant by the soul's learning. When we cease to block the flow by holding on, life becomes light and joyful. One cannot enter the stream of return to the One while holding on or remaining attached to anything on the Earth plane.

I am Dancing Soul
And I will assist you
To untie the knots
That bind you so tightly
To all that is not
Right for you
I will free your
Arms and legs
So that you can
Fly
And I will
Sing with you
Until you have found
Your own song
And should you fall back
To Earth
I will circle the sky above you
And my song
Shall be a beacon
For your soul
Beckoning you
Upwards
For I love you
And am also
Of your essence.

Anger

Expression of anger and rage serves to cleanse people of toxic energies stored within their bodies. This is true at a planetary level as well. When there is imbalance, eventually there must be restoration of balance. Anger, rage and war are the expression of release of toxicity in an unconscious system. In a conscious system negative energies are released in an ongoing way which serves the healthy functioning of the system.

In politics, or relationships, conflict is the result of the refusal of one or both parties to recognize that each is only one part of the system that all have jointly created, and that this system is part of a larger system that was designed to function harmoniously. The illusion of separateness comes in the desire to control, and this control ultimately works against itself. It is like a stranded swimmer fighting against the waves that might otherwise carry him safely to shore.

In trying so hard to control the course of events or behaviors of others, the controller ironically becomes the controlled, for his actions are then not clear responses to the nudgings of the heart, but rather are reactions to something outside of self. All that is needed is to surrender to the ocean of cosmic energies, and to follow the heart, even when the head wants to argue.

I am Dancing Soul
I do not wish
To dance above
The graves
Of war.
We shall warmly
Embrace the souls
Of the innocent
Who return early
To us
For the lessons
Of the Earth
Seem painfully
Slow
And cruel.
You will soon
Know
That even the
Sacrifice of one
Small child's life
Is too high a price
To pay
For global
Unconsciousness.

Loyalty to Essence

First and only loyalty is to essence. When you are loyal and true to your divine essence, you are honoring Source, and all that is. It is beautiful to honor all life and beings, but often this is done with a sense of separateness, as we send love "out there". What is to be honored is the connection, the point at which essence of other flows through self and a sense of oneness is attained, however briefly. We honor the dolphin, or the flower within us, not the image we have projected "out there". It is to allow the merging of essences to experience soul's awareness of its expansiveness.

In the Earth plane there are many lower vibrations, producing negative energy which may unconsciously be taken in or merged with our essence. It is important to become attuned to the subtlety of this energy movement, and to move away from the source of it, and to clear essence as quickly as possible. There is no point in trying to transform that energy, for it cannot be transformed from outside of the being producing it. Attempts to do so only result in your absorbing some of the negative current, which then destabilizes your own higher vibration. If your soul has been affected by such negative energy, you may clear it by going to a peaceful spot, focusing on breathing in clear healing energy, and spending some time in silent meditation. Tune in to your own higher vibrations, and realize that you are not the negative judgements that another may hold of you. Do not stay too long in a job, friendship, or relationship that is dishonoring, because ultimately physical illness may result, and more importantly, in doing so you are not honoring your own essence.

Know as you read this, that you are co-creating the experience that it awakens in you. We serve as a reflection, and desire to touch places in you that may be in darkness. First comes the light, then the dance.

It is with deep love that I honor you.

Solara, assisted by Dancing Soul, who is of my essence.

Harmonic Resonance

There is much joy in our communication with you. We have waited in anticipation of your evolutionary readiness to receive our communication. As your flowers blossom in the warmth of the Sun, so your souls expand into beauty as your vibrations ascend to higher octaves, bathed in the harmony of the Oneness. The Oneness is experienced holographically* when two souls experience resonance. When souls of similar vibration move into resonance, a pattern of the Oneness is created for both, or all, to experience. This is why it is so important to maintain connections with souls whose vibrations resonate with yours. With these individuals you receive your first glimpse of Eternal Love, which is the Love that is Source, and has always been.

---

*Holography, is a form of photography in which a three-dimensional image is recorded on a photographic plate or film by means of laser light. A laser light is split into two beams that interfere with each other to form a pattern which depends on the shape of the photographed object. A three-dimensional image is formed when the photographic plate is exposed to visible light.

In time - actually beyond time - you begin to resonate with this Eternal Love, and this begins to raise the vibrations of other beings on your planet. This resonance does not require physical contact or even physical presence, once you have identified each other as contact points for your excursion into the Beyond. Such presence facilitates and accelerates the process due to the powerful energy currents created, and many, in fact, are somewhat fearful of the power of such energy, as it is a new and different sensation in its intensity. To surrender to it permits great leaps in vibrational levels, but also may disrupt energy flow for these beings. This is not a problem if they are ready to move into expansion, but it is more common on the Earth plane for individuals to experience this energy flow, initially at least, in small doses with space in between. It is also not uncommon for individuals to keep the experience to themselves, and to guard it because they fear that to talk about it may make it disappear. This is how early humans felt about fire when they discovered how to make it happen themselves. At first they felt as though they were playing with something beyond them, perhaps reaching into another dimension, and there was great anxiety about this until creating fire became commonplace. So it is with the meeting of souls whose combined energies allow elevation to, and communication with, other dimensions. But there is really nothing to fear. We hope that you will soon be able to relax and enjoy it!

I am Dancing Soul
And I create
Soft flowing light
To massage your soul
And dances of color
To nurture it.
I merge with your essence
And in harmonizing
With your vibration
Create echoes
Of hauntingly beautiful
Music
Which fills the Universe as a
Significant part of the
Cosmic orchestral performance
Which accompanies
All that is
And travels endlessly
Throughout the Beyond.
I love and honor
Your essence, beloved
The dance is
Ours.

Maintaining the Flow

It is important to follow your intuition and to trust in the divine energies. You are learning to discern the different vibrational levels, and the way in which you have allowed negative vibrations to enter your auric field. Whenever you feel sadness, anger, frustration, or tension, it is because you are out of touch with your own vibration and are tuning into that of others. In higher consciousness, there is only joy and ecstasy, and the understanding that all is happening perfectly.

You need not continue to feel the obligation either to raise the vibrational levels of others or to lower your own to match more closely to theirs. It is fine to be different, and you should celebrate your essence. Looking for acceptance on the Earth plane will only slow your progress. Moving away from those whose vibrations interfere with or negatively affect yours is not to reject them. They too must find their own path. It is most appropriate for you to be with beings who are ready for, and open to you. As you clear obstacles you will find that there is much more waiting for you. Remember to listen to the signals of your body, for it is a sensitively tuned instrument for interpreting vibrational levels around you.

And remember the dance. It is All There Is.

I am Dancing Soul
And never too tired
To dance.
It is
The dance
That energizes
Life and
Soul.
So dance with me
Beloved
You know the
Steps
Of our joy
Our rapture
As we surrender
And die as one
To the love
And the truth.

*So let me
Kiss you
With color
And caress you
With sound
As we spiral up
Towards
The Ultimate
Union.*

EPILOGUE

Imagine your consciousness as a photographic plate onto which the image of wholeness, the Oneness has been recorded. Let the message in this book serve as a visible light, interacting with your consciousness, and allow your awareness to expand infinitely in all directions. Feel the energy in these pages, so that an image forms, far beyond the familiar three-dimensions. This will activate the prior knowing that already exists in your soul. You can tune in to that knowing any time, if you are ready to trust, and to allow yourself to expand your perception of who you are. There is no system to learn, no guru to follow; only the willingness to hear the soulsong that vibrates throughout the Universe as surely as the whalesong resonates throughout the ocean. And when you hear that song, you will know that it is *your* song, and that you have joined the dance.

Journey of my soul's awakening....

OTHER BOOKS BY GWEN RANDALL - YOUNG

ECHOES THROUGH TIME:
A Message of Healing for Men

To Follow:

A Series of Children's Books

Relaxation and Guided Meditation and Healing tapes

For information or comments address:

DANCING SOUL PRODUCTIONS
P.O. Box 80057
Broadmoor P.O.
82 Athabascan Avenue
Sherwood Park, Alberta
Canada T8A 5T1
Phone: (403) 464-8533
FAX: (403) 464-5503

Order Form

Title	Price	Qty.	Total
Dancing Soul: The Voice of Spirit Evolving	Can. - $22 U.S.A - $18		
Echoes Through Time: A Message of Healing for Men	Can. - $22 U.S.A - $18		
		Sub-total	
		Please add 10% for shipping	
		Please add 7% GST	
		TOTAL	

❏ Cheque or money order enclosed.
  Please make cheques payable to <u>DANCING SOUL PRODUCTIONS</u>.

❏ VISA __ __ __ __ / __ __ __ __ / __ __ __ __ / __ __ __ __
  Exp. Date: Mon. ____ Year ____

❏ MASTERCARD __ __ __ __ / __ __ __ __ / __ __ __ __ / __ __ __ __
  Exp. Date: Mon ____ Year ____

SHIP TO:

Name (please print)_____

Street Address_____

City_____ Province/State _____

Postal/Zip Code _____

Phone: Day (___)_____ Evening (___)_____

Please allow 4 to 6 weeks delivery.
For rush orders please call 403-464-8533 and use Mastercard or Visa.

DANCING SOUL PRODUCTIONS
A Division of Gwen Randall-Young
Psychological Services Ltd.
P.O. 80057
Broadmoor P.O.
82 Athabascan Ave.
Sherwood Park, Alberta
Canada T8A 5T1
Phone: (403) 464-8533 FAX: (403) 464-5503